COLLECTIONS

A Harcourt Reading / Language Arts Program

DECODABLE BOOK
BOOK 1-5

Harcourt

Orlando   Boston   Dallas   Chicago   San Diego

Visit *The Learning Site!*

www.hbschool.com

Contents

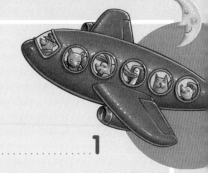

TRAVEL TIPS

by
Susan Blackaby

illustrated by
Tracy Sabin

You might travel by car.
Stopping for snacks is fun.

**Seeing the sights by bike
is fun, too.**

3

Travel by bus and see the sights while eating lunch.

4

A night flight on a jet is fun.
See all the bright lights as
you fly high in the sky.

Take your time and cross the
high seas by ship. It's nice
in the bright sun.

6

It's best to pack light!
You might get stuck in
a tight spot.

Traveling might be fun,
but getting back home
is nice, too!

8

THE Helping Day

by
Donna Taylor

illustrated by
Mike Reed

One rainy day, Mom had a
bad cold. "I think it is best
if you stay inside and play,"
said Mom.
"We will, Mom," said Taylor
and Gail.

"Let's help Mom feel better,"
said Taylor. Taylor set toast
and milk on Mom's tray.

On the way, the tray went plop! Bang! Taylor and Gail grabbed the mop.

"Let's make get-well cards for Mom," called Gail. "It will be mail for Mom." Gail got crayons, markers, and paint.

13

The paints went splat! What a mess! Taylor and Gail grabbed the mop.

14

"This is a better way," said
Taylor. "We will bring the mail.
This is a letter that will
stay on!"

"Oh, my! What a gift for the
day!" giggled Mom. "You have
brightened up this gray,
rainy day!"

Hi, Green Beans!

by Mary Hogan
illustrated by Casey Craig

It's spring, and it's sunny
and mild. It's garden time!

18

I'll plant green beans. I'll find a nice spot with lots of sunlight.

19

I dig holes two inches deep
and plant my seeds. I don't
mind getting dirty.

Rain falls. It makes the seeds
grow bigger and bigger.

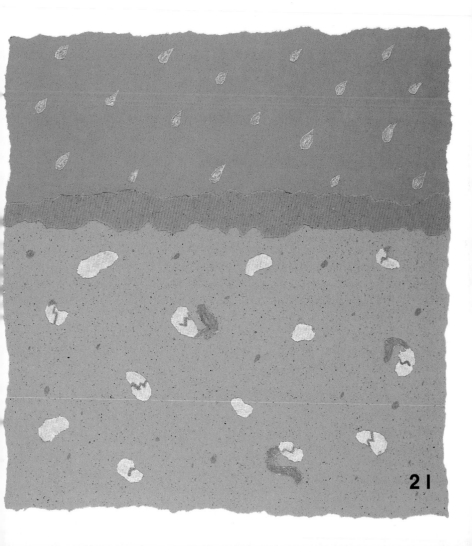

Stems rise. Small leaves grow
on the stems. Sunshine will
make the plants grow tall.

22

I see beetles munching on my plants. Scat, beetles! Find some other kind of lunch.

I wait and wait. At last I can say, "Hi, green beans!"

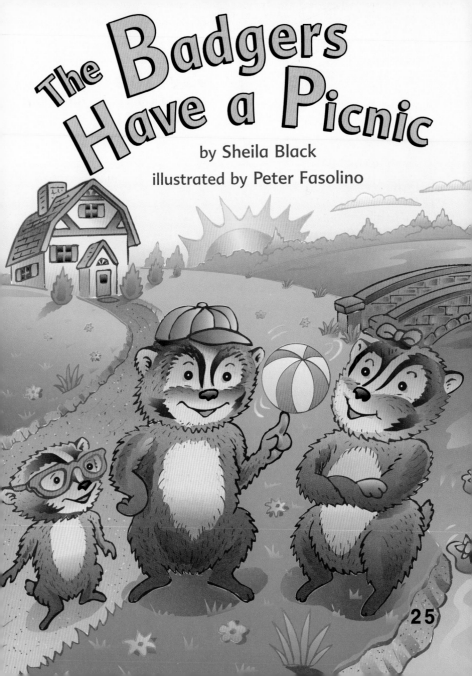

The Badgers Have a Picnic

by Sheila Black

illustrated by Peter Fasolino

"Let's have a picnic," said Jack. "We'll sit by the bridge at Dodge Lake."

26

"I'll help!" yelled Madge. Jack sniffed. "You're much too little to help."

"I'll pack ginger snaps and this large wedge of fudge," Ginny chirped.

28

"We'll get sick if we eat
just that!" cried Jack. "I'll
pack orange salad and
sandwiches."

"We forgot something," Ginny grumbled.
"Is it this wedge of cheese?" asked Jack.

30

"It's the basket!" Ginny
cried. "We need the
picnic basket!"

Madge smiled a big, big smile. "Here it is!" she giggled. "See? I can help!"

Let's Go!

by Anne Miranda
illustrated by Jesse Reisch

"Let's go," said Mom.

34

"No," Jo moaned. "That wind is cold. I don't like snow! The last time we went out, my nose froze."

"Oh, Jo," Mom sighed.
"Bundle up. We'll have fun!"

Jo bundled up, and so did
Mom. "Let's go," called Mom.
"We'll make snow prints!"

"This snow is so fluffy,"
Jo said.
"Now let's skate," said
Mom.

"The last time, I fell," Jo
grumbled. "I bet I will fall
again."
"No, you won't," groaned
Mom. "Hold my hand.
Let's go!"

"This is fun!" Jo cried.
"I told you so!"
laughed Mom.

40

Queen June and the Rude Duke

by J.C. Cunningham
illustrated by Chris Lensch

Once upon a time, there was a queen named June. Queen June had the best manners.

She would always say please
and thanks. She never, ever
played silly tricks.

One day, Duke Bruce
came to visit. Duke Bruce
was quite cute, but he had
bad, bad manners.

44

Duke Bruce would never, ever say please or thanks. He liked playing silly tricks.

One night, Queen June gave a
huge ball. A big band played
dance tunes. Duke Bruce acted
so silly!

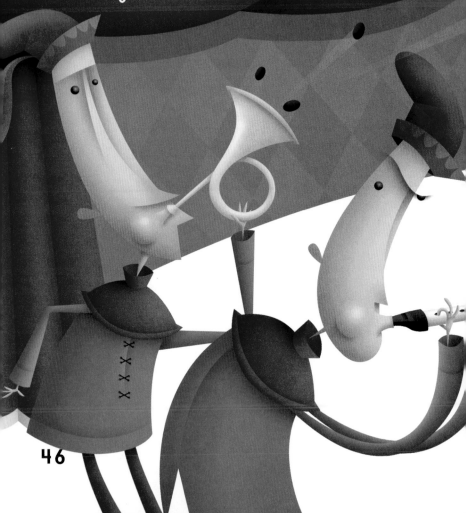

He stuffed prunes in all the flutes! He filled Queen June's crown with ice cubes!

47

Rude Duke Bruce
was never seen again.

48

Ned's Feathers

by
Betsy Franco

illustrated by
Loretta Lustig

Ned fluffed his feathers. He was ready to go shopping.

Ned skipped down Meadow Road.
"I think I'll get bread," he mumbled.

After shopping, the weather got bad. "I won't take that long way," said Ned.

"Instead, this shortcut home will be fine."

"Yum!" cried Fox as she spotted
Ned. "A sandwich for lunch!"

Ned wasn't going to be Fox's lunch.
That wouldn't be pleasant!

"My, my! All those eyes!" Fox screamed. Ned just smiled and headed home.